GeoTrivia BODY

MW00845340

Illustrated by Susan Jacoby

CONTENTS

The Inside Scoop!

What's in the book?

What's on the pages?

 **MiNd BeNders**

Mindbending questions—Test your knowledge, quiz your friends, and stump the grown-ups!

AnSwers

Correct and clever answers—Use the MINDBENDER ANSWER FLAP on the back cover to hide them. (Don't peek!)

GEO-TIP *Helpful hints—Keep these handy to help you remember what's what in the body!*

Geo-Challenge

Experiments to test your body IQ— Take the challenge if you dare!

Top Trivia

▶ *The biggest,*
▶ *smallest,*
▶ *longest,*
▶ *lightest,*
▶ *heaviest body trivia ever—*
▶ *Make a quest through the "-ests"!*

 **AMAZING FACTS**

Fun and fascinating bits of information—

Amaze your friends and family with your body knowledge!

Body Map

Where It's At

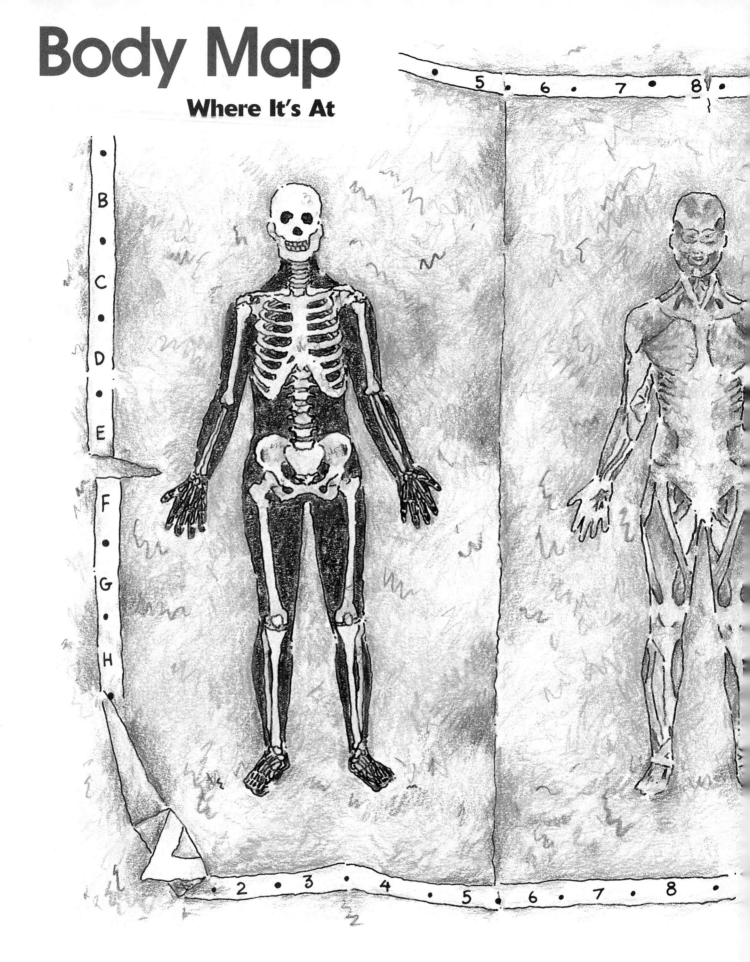

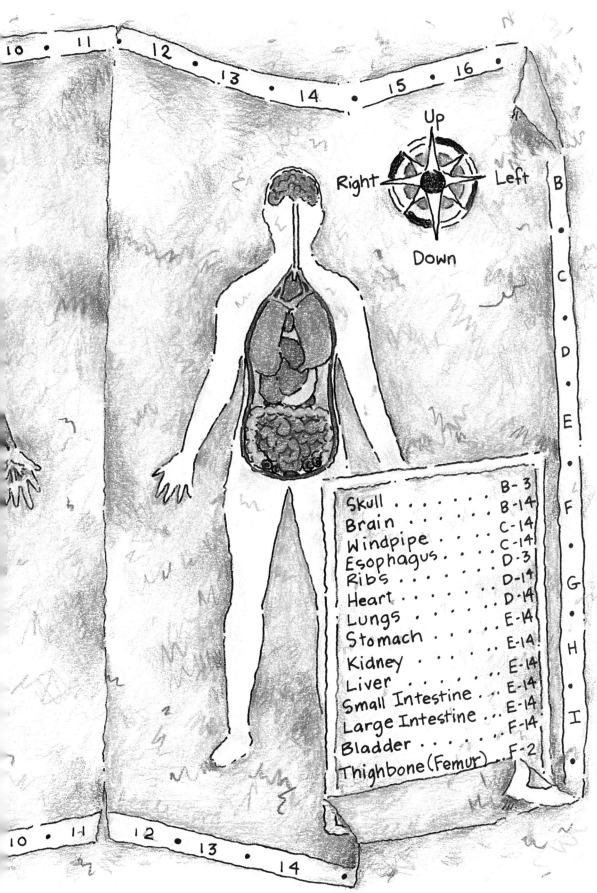

Skull	B-3
Brain	B-14
Windpipe	C-14
Esophagus	C-14
Ribs	D-3
Heart	D-14
Lungs	D-14
Stomach	E-14
Kidney	E-14
Liver	E-14
Small Intestine	E-14
Large Intestine	E-14
Bladder	F-14
Thighbone (Femur)	F-2

What's with the compass? The right and left look all mixed up!
Think of it this way—if you're facing someone, that person's
right side is on your left side. That's why the compass is reversed.

Building Blocks
A Cell-a-bration of Life

Mind Benders

1. True or false? All living things, including the human body, are made up of cells.

2. Choose one. Would you use a telescope, microscope, or periscope to see most cells up close?

3. Do all cells look alike?

4. Which is NOT a kind of cell you would find in your body—blood cells, bone cells, jail cells, or muscle cells?

5. True or false? All cells live about a week and then are replaced by new ones.

6. How are new cells made? (GEO-HINT: The cells are *divided* over this answer.)

7. What runs the cell—the nucleus, chief organelle, or head cellmaster?

8. Does the cell membrane (outer layer) let food and oxygen in or does it let waste out?

9. The cell's mitochondria are like power stations. Do they change food into energy or juice?

10. True or false? Your cells stop dividing when you are about 21 years old.

11. When lots of similar cells join together do they form cellophane or tissue?

AMAZING FACTS

Your body is made up of about 75 trillion cells. (Give or take a hundred million!)

You could fit a row of about 40 brain cells (the smallest cells of all) across the dot of an *i*.

Why doesn't a haircut hurt? Because your hair is actually made of dead cells! (Talk about a bad hair day!)

DANGER!
TISSUE UNDER CONSTRUCTION

Answers

1. True

2. Microscope—Because they're so tiny!

3. No—They come in many shapes and sizes. (Each type of cell has a different job to do.)

4. Jail cells (Some people might find their bodies in a jail cell, but they'd never find a jail cell in their bodies!)

5. False—Some cells, like nerve cells, last a lifetime, while others, like skin cells, survive only a few days.

6. Living cells split, or divide in two, to make new cells—This is called mitosis.

See ya' later!

7. The nucleus

8. Trick question—It does both.

9. Energy

10. False—Many cells keep dividing and making new cells your whole life.

11. Tissue—Tissue is made of many building blocks, or cells. (Sort of the way a house is made of bricks.)

Bones & Muscles
Shake, Rattle, and Roll!

Mind Benders

1. How many bones are in your body—about 100, 200, or 400?

2. Your bones form your body's frame. What's this frame called? (GEO-HINT: There's one on the cover of this book, and you might see a few on Halloween, too.)

3. Choose one. Are your bones linked together by joints, screws, or glue?

4. True or false? Your backbone, or spine, is made up of one very long bone.

5. There's a protective "cage" around your lungs and heart. What's the name of this "cage"?

6. True or false? Nearly half of the bones in your entire body are located in your hands and feet.

7. Do you have more bones or muscles?

8. You have three different kinds of muscles in your body. Which of these is NOT a kind of muscle—smooth, rough, cardiac, or skeletal?

9. True or false? All muscles are voluntary, moving only when you want them to.

10. You just kicked a soccer ball. Are your leg muscles pulling or pushing?

11. True or false? The more you use your muscles, the bigger and stronger they get.

Top Trivia

▶ The longest and strongest bone in your body is the bone that runs from your hip to your knee. It's called the femur.

▶ The smallest bones are in your ear. They're called the hammer, anvil, and stirrup, and all together are only about the size of a dime. (Maybe hearing should be the "tenth sense"!)

▶ The strongest muscles in your body are your masseters, which help you bite and chew. (Chow down!)

AMAZING FACTS

Ever heard the term double-jointed? There is really no such thing. People who seem double-jointed just have very flexible ligaments.

Bone dry? Not so! About ¼ of each of your bones is water.

Can you wiggle your ears? You have muscles for wiggling your ears, but you probably never use them, so they weaken from lack of use.

Answers

1. About 200—206 to be exact! (Although some people have an extra pair of ribs.)

2. Skeleton—Your skeleton gives you shape and protects your organs.

3. Joints

4. False—There are 33 bones, or vertebrae, in your spine! (Your spine can really bend over backwards for you!)

5. Rib cage

6. True

7. Muscles—About 650 of them!

8. Rough—Smooth muscles help your body's internal systems, cardiac muscles make up your heart, and skeletal muscles are connected to your bones to help you move.

9. False—Some muscles are, but other muscles are involuntary and work automatically. (Imagine if you had to think about making your heart beat!)

10. Pulling, or contracting—Muscles never push; they only contract or relax.

11. True

Inside & Out
Internal Organs and Skin

1. Are organs made up of tissues or cells?

2. True or false? Organs are parts of your body that have particular jobs to do.

3. Some of your organs come in twos. Which of these organs is NOT part of a pair—lung, liver, or kidney?

4. Can you name the organ that has many folds and fits inside your skull? (GEO-HINT: *Think* about it!)

5. Could you survive without your appendix?

6. Take your pulse. What internal organ are you checking on?

7. What do you call the organ that stirs and mashes food—your jaw, stomach, or organ grinder?

8. As you read this question, which organs help you see the words and understand what they mean?

9. Are kidneys shaped like beans, rice, or gumballs?

10. You just did a backbend. Did your skin stretch?

11. True or false? Identical twins have the exact same fingerprints.

12. Are organs that work together called systems, networks, or teams?

Geo-Challenge

Grab a tennis ball and give it a good hard squeeze. This is how strongly your heart delivers one pump, or beat. Try squeezing and releasing 70 times in a minute. How does your hand feel? Your heart is one strong muscle, isn't it?

ORGAN-IZED!

Top Trivia

▶ *The hottest part of your whole body is the center of your brain. The coolest parts of your body are your fingers and toes.*

▶ *What's your body's largest organ? Your skin. (You're surrounded by it!)*

▶ *The left kidney is higher because the liver presses the right kidney down a bit. (The liver is so pushy!)*

Answers

1. Trick question, both—Cells group together to form tissue; then tissues group together to form organs.

2. True

3. Liver

4. Your brain

5. Yes

6. Your heart (Did you get the beat?)

7. Stomach—Your jaw is not an organ, and an organ grinder is a muscian!

8. Your eyes and your brain—Your eyes take the information in, but your brain interprets the message!

9. Beans (So, which came first, the kidney bean or the kidney?)

10. Yes—Whenever you move a body part, your skin must stretch.

11. False—No two fingerprints are the same!

12. Systems

BRAIN POWER
The Control Center

Mind Benders

1. Is your brain a part of your nervous system or respiratory system?

2. Your brain is made up of three main parts. Which of the following is NOT one of them—the cerebrum, cerebellum, microchip, or brain stem?

3. Is your brain wrinkled and soft or smooth and hard?

4. Choose one. What part of your body protects your brain—your skull, skin, hair, or all three?

5. True or false? Different parts of your brain do different jobs.

6. Your brain is divided into hemispheres. Does hemisphere mean "half" or "quarter"?

7. True or false? The right side of your brain controls the right side of your body.

8. If your brain were a computer, would it be turned off while you're sleeping?

9. Do "brainy" kids have bigger brains?

10. True or false? Your brain reaches its full weight when you are 16 years old.

11. Is "brainstorming" good for problem solving or getting rid of a headache?

fly buzzing near ear... ...send hand up to swat...

Geo-Challenge

How's your short-term memory? Look at the ten items pictured below for one minute. Now close the book and see how many you can remember.

Answers

1. Nervous system

2. Microchip

3. Wrinkled and soft

4. All three—Your brain is so important that it needs all the protection it can get. (That's why you wear a helmet for many sports!)

5. True—There are areas of your brain that control things like thinking, hearing, talking, running, and remembering.

6. "Half"—Your brain has two sides, right and left.

7. False—The right side of your brain controls the left side of your body, and the left side of your brain controls the right side of your body. (Are your wires getting crossed?)

8. No—Your brain needs to be "on" so it can do things like keep your heart beating, help you breathe, and help you dream. (Maybe your brain should be called a "dream machine"!)

9. No—Usually the size of your brain does not affect how smart you are.

10. False—Your brain reaches its full weight when you are about 6 years old.

11. Problem solving

AMAZING FACTS

About 80% of your brain is water.

Your brain gets more messages from your fingers than it does from your arms and legs combined.

Are you right-handed or left-handed? For right-handed people, the left side of the brain controls language and math skills and the right side controls creative skills. For lefties, it's exactly the opposite. (Got that?)

You've Got Some Nerve!

The Nervous System

Mind Benders

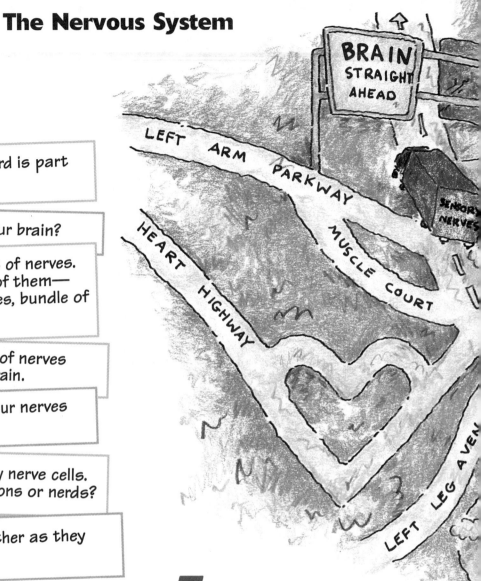

1. True or false? Your spinal cord is part of your nervous system.

2. Are nerves found only in your brain?

3. You have two different kinds of nerves. Which of these is NOT one of them—sensory nerves, motor nerves, bundle of nerves?

4. True or false? Both kinds of nerves carry messages to the brain.

5. When you are nervous, do your nerves tie up in knots?

6. Nerves are made up of tiny nerve cells. Are these cells called neurons or nerds?

7. Do nerve cells touch each other as they pass messages?

8. Choose one. What protects the thick bundle of nerves that make up your spinal cord—your vertebrae, ribs, or brain stem?

9. True or false? When you touch a hot stove your nerves must carry a message through your spinal cord to your brain before you can move your hand.

10. Which of these is NOT a reflex action—sneezing, singing, or shivering?

11. It takes a lot of nerve to skydive. Does that mean skydivers have more nerve cells than the average person?

Top Trivia

▶ The longest cells in your body are the neurons in your nervous system, which measure in at about 4 feet (1.3 meters).

▶ About 30,000 miles (48,000 kilometers) of nerves weave through your body. If your nerves were connected to make a superhighway, this nervy road would be long enough to go all the way around the planet Neptune.

▶ The thickest parts of your spinal cord are in your neck and lower back. That's because so many nerves go to your arms and legs.

Answers

1. True—The other parts of your nervous system are your brain and nerves.

2. No—A network of nerves branches out all over your body. (Talk about an internet!)

3. Bundle of nerves—That's just a saying that means "very nervous."

4. False—Sensory nerves carry messages from your sense organs to your brain, and the motor nerves carry messages from your brain to your muscles.

5. No, it only feels that way! (Relax!)

6. Neurons

7. No—There is a small gap called a synapse between nerve cells. Messages "jump" from cell to cell.

8. Your vertebrae, or backbone

9. False—To keep you from burning yourself, your spinal cord sends a quick message to your muscles making you move your hand. At the same time, a message goes to your brain telling you you're in pain. This is called a reflex.

10. Singing—A reflex action is something you do automatically without thinking about it.

11. No (But they sure have more guts!)

Take a Breather
The Respiratory System

Mind Benders

1. Does respiration mean "breathing" or "sweating"?

2. Which of these is NOT part of the respiratory system—nose, throat, windpipe, windsock, or lungs?

3. What is the main entrance to your respiratory system? (GEO-HINT: It smells.)

4. True or false? Sometimes people forget to breathe.

5. When you inhale, or breathe in, are you filling your lungs with oxygen or carbon dioxide?

6. True or false? Your lungs send oxygen into your blood to be carried throughout your body.

7. Are both your lungs the same size?

8. Do you breathe faster when you are resting or running?

9. Can you really see your breath on a cold day?

10. Do you need your lungs to talk?

11. Is your voice box (larnyx) really a box?

BREATHE IN...

... BREATHE OUT

GEO-TIP *The insides of your lungs look like upside-down trees. The main **Trunk** is your **Trachea** (windpipe) and the **Branches** are the **Bronchi** and **Bronchioles**. At the end of the bronchioles are air sacs called alveoli.*

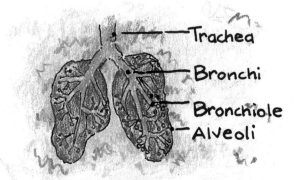

Trachea
Bronchi
Bronchiole
Alveoli

Answers

1. "Breathing"

2. Windsock

3. Your nose—Your mouth is also an entrance, but you usually breathe through your nose.

4. False—You can't forget because a special area of your brain reminds you. (So don't even think about it!)

5. Oxygen—You exhale, or breathe out, carbon dioxide.

6. True

7. No—Your right lung has three lobes, or sections, but your left lung has only two, to make room for your heart.

8. Running—When you use more energy, your muscles need more oxygen.

9. Yes—The air you breathe out has water vapor in it, which condenses and looks like a little puff of steam.

10. You sure do!—And you need your voice box (larnyx), too.

11. No—It's the place in your throat where sounds are made. (It's sometimes called your Adam's Apple, too.)

AMAZING FACTS

In your whole body, there is only one organ light enough to float on water—your air-filled lungs.

You can live a few days without water and even longer without food, but you can't live without oxygen for more than a few minutes.

Let's Circulate!
The Circulatory System

Mind Benders

1. True or false? Blood supplies your body's tissues and muscles with food and oxygen.

2. What shape does the word *circulatory* remind you of?

3. Which of your body's organs sends blood throughout your body?

4. True or false? Blood gets around to all parts of the body by flowing through "tubes," or vessels, called arteries, capillaries, and veins.

5. Choose one. Is your heart like a pump, fan, or hose?

6. Is your heart really heart-shaped?

7. Point to your heart. Did you point to the right, left, or middle of your chest?

8. Is the yellowish liquid that makes up just over half of your blood called platelets, plasma, or plaque?

9. True or false? Your blood has red, white, and blue cells.

10. Do red or white blood cells help your body fight off disease?

11. Does your heart beat faster or slower when you're playing sports?

12. You exercise your leg muscles when you jog or ride a bike. Are you also exercising your heart?

Geo-Challenge

Blood flows against gravity in some parts of the body. To test this, raise one arm above your head. Keep the other arm down at your side. Hold this position for a minute and then compare hands. Your lowered hand should be darker because the blood has to force its way upward against gravity.

Top Trivia

▶ A heart beats more than 2 billion times during the average lifetime. (But who's counting?)

▶ There are four blood types—A, B, AB, and O. The most common is O; the least common is AB. (Which type are you?)

▶ Most men have more blood in their bodies than women—about one quart (one liter) more.

Answers

1. True—Blood also carries away waste. (Talk about a delivery and pick-up service!)

2. A circle—Blood circles, or circulates, throughout your body. (That's why it's called the circulatory system!)

3. The heart (Don't be heartbroken if you missed this one!)

4. True

5. A pump—It actually has two sides, one that pumps blood to your lungs and another that sends blood to the rest of your body.

6. No—It's really shaped like a fist. (And it's about the same size, too.)

7. The middle (Although most of it is on the left side.)

8. Plasma—The other part of blood is made up of floating cells.

9. False—Your blood doesn't have blue cells.

10. White cells—They protect your body against invading germs.

11. Faster—To send extra blood and oxygen to your muscles

12. Yes!—When your heart beats harder and faster, your heart muscle becomes stronger.

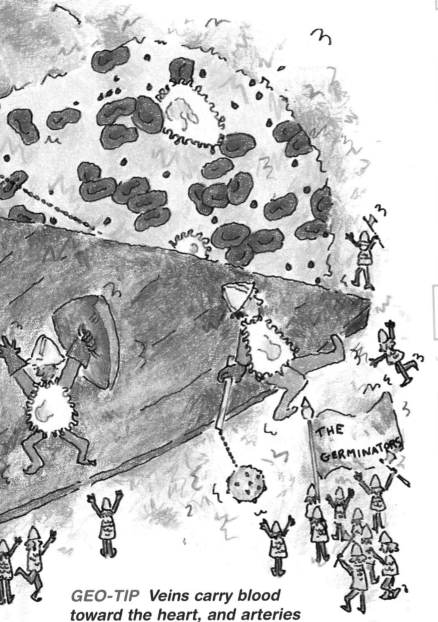

THE GERMINATORS

GEO-TIP Veins carry blood toward the heart, and arteries carry blood away from the heart. Here's a simple rhyme to help you remember—*Artery* and *Away* both start with **A**.

what do you call two fighting valentines? ...a heart attack!

19

Eaters' Digest

The Digestive System

Mind Benders

1. Your body breaks down food so that it's small enough to enter your cells. Is this process called digestion, indigestion, or chowing down?

2. Which organ is NOT part of the digestive system—your mouth, stomach, small intestine, large intestine, or bladder?

3. True or false? Digestion begins before you start eating.

4. Choose one. What do you call the area of your brain that tells you you're hungry—the snack bar, appetite center, or hamburger joint?

5. Your teeth help you chew. Does your tongue help, too?

6. Does food go down your esophagus or your windpipe?

7. Can you swallow food while you're standing on your head?

8. Where is your stomach—above, below, or behind your ribs?

9. True or false? The greatest amount of digestion occurs when food is in your stomach.

10. Which of these organs helps you digest food when it's in your small intestine—liver, gall bladder, pancreas, or all three?

11. True or false? The longest part of your body is the digestive tract.

AMAZING FACTS

Your body produces about 5 cups of saliva each day. (That's a lot of spit!)

Can you imagine eating 40 tons of food? This is the amount of grub an average American eats in a lifetime. (What a mouthful!)

Believe it or not, straight stomach acid could burn a hole in wool carpeting. Luckily, this acid makes up only a tiny part of your stomach's juices, and the stomach walls are protected by a coating of thick, slimy mucus.

Answers

1. Digestion

2. Bladder

3. True—As soon as you see and smell food, your mouth starts making saliva, which is the liquid that helps break down food. (Talk about a mouth-watering meal!)

4. Appetite center

5. Yes—Your tongue moves food around in your mouth and helps push food to the back of your throat so you can swallow it.

6. Your esophagus—Your windpipe carries air in and out of your lungs.

7. Yes—Muscles in your esophagus squeeze food through to your stomach. (But, eating upside-down isn't such a great idea—you could choke!)

8. Behind (Although many people think it's *below* the ribs.)

9. False—Some digestion does take place in your stomach, but the greatest amount occurs when food is moving through your small intestine.

10. All three—Bile from the liver, and gall bladder and pancreatic juices mix with food to break it down into even smaller pieces.

11. True—if it were straightened out, you would have to be taller than a giraffe for it to fit in your body.

21

The Fabulous Five

Your Senses

Mind Benders

1. Can you name your body's five main senses?

2. Is the colored part of your eye called the iris, pupil, or student?

3. You just walked into a very dark room. Did your pupils get bigger or smaller?

4. Does binocular vision mean you can see things with both eyes at once or that you can see things that are very far away?

5. If you're walking on a balance beam, do your ears or nose help you keep your balance?

6. Are there any sounds you can't hear?

7. Can loud noises really damage your hearing?

8. How many different smells can most people smell—about 4,000 or 40,000?

9. True or false? The longer you smell a bad odor, the worse it gets.

10. There are four main tastes. Which of the following is NOT one of them— sweet, salty, slimy, bitter, or sour?

11. You're about to bite into a slice of pizza. Which senses will work together to help you enjoy it?

12. Your sense of touch includes everything you can feel with your skin. Which of these is NOT one of those things—heat, cold, color, or pain?

? Geo-Challenge

Make up your own touch test. Gather a bunch of stuff, like cotton balls, rocks, paper clips, small toys, cold spaghetti, or anything else you can dig up—be creative. Then get some volunteers to take this test. Blindfold them and ask them to figure out what each thing is by touch alone. (No peeking!)

Answers

1. Sight, hearing, smell, taste, and touch

2. The iris (The *pupil* is the black part in the center of your iris, and a *student* is . . . well, you know!)

3. Bigger—To let more light in so you can see better

4. You can see things with both eyes at once

5. Ears—There's fluid in your semicircular canals that moves around and helps keep you level.

6. Yes—People are not able to hear really high frequency sounds. (But dogs can!)

7. Yes! (Aspiring rock stars and construction workers beware!)

8. About 4,000 (People with really sensitive noses can smell about 10,000.)

9. False—Your nose gets used to any smell the longer you smell it.

10. Slimy—*Slimy* is a texture, not a taste. (Gross!)

11. Taste, sight, and smell—Taste is the weakest of all your senses. Your brain needs input from your nose, eyes, and tongue to taste things.

12. Color—Other things you can feel are pressure and texture.

Top Trivia

▶ **No two irises (the colored part of your eye) are alike. In fact, your iris is even more unique than your fingerprint. Look in the mirror to "EYE-dentify" the patterns of spots, lines, and swirls in your own baby blues, browns, or greens.**

▶ **Did you know that more men than women are color-blind? (They can't see certain colors—usually red and green.) It's true! If you took a group of 200 men and a group of 200 women, about 16 of the men would be color blind, but only 1 of the women would be!**

Growing Up

Here's Looking At You, Kid!

Mind Benders

1. You could recognize your mom almost immediately after you were born. Did you know her by the way she looked or smelled?

2. Did you flash your first gummy smile when you were about six weeks old or six months old?

3. True or false? You couldn't communicate until you learned to talk.

4. Choose one. At what age do people grow the most—between 0–2, 8–10, or 18–20 years?

5. Is a toddler older than an adolescent?

6. Does everybody need the same amount of sleep each day?

7. At what age does a tike learn to ride a trike—three years old or five years old? (GEO-HINT: How old were you when you learned to ride a three-wheeler?)

8. Which of these is NOT a kind of tooth—baby tooth, permanent tooth, wisdom tooth, or sweet tooth?

9. Are most kids about four or six years old when their baby teeth start falling out?

10. When is your eyesight the best—when you're about 8, 28, or 48 years old?

11. Can you tell how tall you'll be when you grow up?

1. By the way she smelled—Your eyesight wasn't that great when you were a newborn.

2. About six weeks old

3. False—You cried when you were a baby to tell others things like "I'm hungry" and "I'm sleepy."

4. 0–2 years

5. No—Adolescents are teenagers and toddlers are children who are beginning to learn how to walk.

6. No—Babies need the most and older adults need the least amount of sleep each day.

7. Three-year-old tikes ride three-wheeler bikes!

8. Sweet tooth—Having a "sweet tooth" just means you like eating sweet foods like candy and cookies. (Yum!)

9. About six years old

10. About eight years old

11. Yes—Boys are ¾ their adult height at about 9 years old. Girls are ¾ their adult height at about 7 ½ years old. (How tall will you be when you grow up?)

AMAZING FACTS

At birth, you had about 350 bones. By the time you're fully grown, you'll have about 206. How can that be? Bones join together, or fuse, as you grow older.

Most people have 20 baby teeth and 32 permanent teeth. But some people's "permanent" teeth aren't really permanent. They lose that set of teeth and actually grow a third set!

Eat Smart, Play Hard

Nutrition and Exercise

Mind Benders

1. True or false? Food is to your body like gasoline is to a car.

2. Is the amount of energy in food measured in calories or kilowats?

3. Do you gain or lose weight when you eat more calories than you burn off?

4. True or false? Experts say a balanced diet is made up of carbohydrates, protein, and fats.

5. Choose one. Do people get vitamins, minerals, or both from foods?

6. True or false? Fiber isn't good for your body because you can't digest it.

7. Choose one. Is junk food scraps of leftovers or food with little nutritional value?

8. If you're trying to eat healthy food, would you follow the food square, pyramid, or circle?

9. Which weighs more—fat or muscle?

10. Is it important to warm up before exercising?

11. Aerobic exercises give your heart and lungs a good workout. Which is NOT an aerobic exercise—dancing, golfing, or cross-country skiing?

12. You're playing tennis on a hot day. Should you drink water or take a shower to replace the fluids you've lost?

Top Trivia

▶ The tallest corn in the U.S. grew to 31 feet (9.4 meters). That's taller than four NBA basketball players standing on one another's shoulders!

▶ The longest lima bean in the U.S. was 14 inches (36 centimeters) long. (Imagine trying to hide that lima bean under your mashed potatoes!)

AMAZING FACTS

Bikers and hikers carry high-energy snacks that they can eat in a hurry. One of those snacks is called "gorp," which stands for *Good Old Raisins and Peanuts!*

You're supposed to drink about 8 glasses of water a day. That's more than 180 gallons a year, or enough to fill about 5 bathtubs!

Answers

1. True—Food is your body's fuel. Your body turns that fuel into energy to keep you going.

2. Calories

3. You gain weight

4. True (You hear a lot of bad stuff about fat these days, but you do need some.)

5. Both—Vitamins and minerals are important nutrients that help keep you healthy.

6. False—Even though you can't digest fiber, it's good for you because it helps your body get rid of waste.

7. Food with little nutritional value

8. Food pyramid—It shows how many daily servings of fruits and veggies, dairy, and all that other good stuff you should eat.

9. Muscle (That's why strong people can really throw their weight around!)

10. Yes—To get your body stretched and loose so you won't hurt yourself.

11. Golfing (For an exercise to be aerobic, you have to do it continuously—and at a good pace—for at least 20 minutes.)

12. Drink some water or a sports drink (A shower might feel good, but it can't replace the water your body loses when you sweat.)

Why Do I...?

The Body's Oddities

1. When you sneeze, is your nose acting like a vacuum cleaner, a snow blower, or a blender?

2. You just drank a whole can of soda pop in three gulps. Now what are you most likely to do—yawn, cough, or burp?

3. Does your stomach "growl" only when you're hungry?

4. Your foot fell asleep and it feels like "pins and needles." Is this feeling caused by tired muscles or blood rushing back to your foot?

5. It's raining, it's pouring, the old man is snoring. Is he sleeping with his mouth open or closed?

6. True or false? When you shiver, your muscles are moving back and forth to make heat.

7. You're watching a scary movie, and your body starts to tense up. Do your tightened muscles give you goose bumps or a charley horse?

8. What are your body's windshield wipers? (GEO-HINT: You should get this answer in the *blink* of an eye.)

9. True or false? Your fingers and toes get wrinkled when you take a bath because they're dry.

10. Is your funny bone *really* a bone?

11. Why do you sweat—to warm up, cool down, or dry off?

where do your bones meet?

Geo-Challenge

Yawning is contagious, but we really don't know why. Try this experiment the next time you're with a group of friends or family—start yawning to see if anyone "catches" a yawn from you.

AMAZING FACTS

For more than 69 years an Iowa man hiccupped every 1½ seconds! (What's *your* trick for getting rid of the hiccups?)

How fast is a sneeze? Faster than a speeding car! You sneeze at almost 100 mph (160 kph).

...at all kinds of joints!

Grrr....

Answers

1. A snow blower—Sneezing clears your nasal passages by blasting dirt and dust out of your nose.

2. Burp (Excuse me!)

3. No—It "growls" all the time because it's always churning. It's probably loudest, though, when empty.

4. Blood rushing back to your foot—When blood begins to flow again, nerves start screaming messages to your brain. All the sudden activity gives your foot that prickly feeling.

5. Open

6. True (Shivering is a great way to warm up without using a lot of energy.)

7. Goose bumps—Your hair stands straight up, giving you bumps that look like the skin on a plucked goose!

8. Your eyelids—When you blink, your eyelids spread tear fluid over your eyes washing away dirt and killing germs.

9. Believe it or not, it's true!—Even though you're surrounded by wet water it's actually pulling the moisture right out of your skin.

10. No—Your funny bone is a nerve that runs from your shoulder all the way down to your pinkie. (Bumping your funny bone is no joke!)

11. To cool down—When sweat evaporates it makes you feel cooler.

The Adaptable Body
Geography and You

1. You're climbing Alaska's Mount McKinley. Are you breathing more times per minute than you would at sea level?

2. Would you worry about frostbite or heat stroke if you were going to Antarctica?

3. Choose one. If you're on an airplane, might your ears snap, pop, or crack?

4. You're deep-sea diving in the Pacific Ocean. To keep from getting the "bends," should you rise to the water's surface quickly or slowly?

5. If you want to visit Death Valley, California, where temperatures can reach 125° F (52° C), should you bring along a canteen or some eggs?

6. Can you get motion sickness while traveling on the ocean?

7. Because people in Norway don't see the sun for two months in winter, some of them get the doldrums. Is this condition called SAD, MAD, or GLAD?

8. You just flew from London to Chicago. Are you likely to get jet lag?

9. If you blasted into space, would your body get taller or shorter?

10. You've made it to the moon. Do you weigh more or less than you did on earth?

GEO-TIP *Wearing light-colored clothing will keep you cooler when it's hot outside. Light colors reflect the sun's heat, while dark colors absorb it.*

AMAZING FACTS

People who live in the Sahara beat the heat by traveling through the desert at night when temperatures are much cooler.

Can't float? Take a dip in the Great Salt Lake in Utah. With all that salt you'll have a hard time doing anything but float.

Here's a hot one! In 1960, members of the U.S. Air Force did some tests to see how high a temperature they could stand. With their clothes on, the highest dry-air temperature they could stand was 500° F (260° C). Without their clothes, it was 400° F (205° C). Ouch!

Answers

1. Yes—The air at high altitudes has less oxygen than it does at sea level, so you will breathe faster.

2. Frostbite—Antarctica is the coldest continent on Earth.

3. Pop—But they don't actually "pop." What sounds like popping is really your Eustachian tubes clearing.

4. Very slowly—The bends, or decompression sickness, is caused when a diver rises too quickly and gets nitrogen bubbles in his or her blood.

5. Bring a canteen filled with plenty of water to replace the water you lose through sweating. (Although you could cook the eggs on a rock!)

6. Sure—Another name for motion sickness is "sea sick," which you might also get in a car or airplane.

7. SAD, which stands for Seasonal Affective Disorder

8. Yes—Because you've crossed a few time zones, you'll need a day or so to get your body clock set on Chicago time.

9. Taller—The lack of gravity in space would make the bones in your spine spread out, so you'd grow about an inch.

10. Less—Because the moon has about six times less gravity than the earth.

THE END

Just for the Fun of It!

Geo Jokes

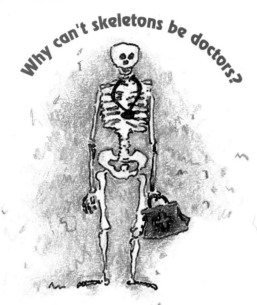

Why can't skeletons be doctors?

They have no stomach for it.

What vitamin should you take if you want better eyesight?

Vitamin See

If buttercups are yellow, what color are hiccups?

Burple

What makes the Tower of Pisa *lean*?

It doesn't eat very much.

What can you find on every vampire's table?

Platelets

How many ears did Davy Crockett have?

Three—a right ear, a left ear, and a wild frontier